EXTINCT

EXTINCT

LISOWICIA

Ben Garrod

Illustrated by Gabriel Ugueto

ZEPHYR

An imprint of Head of Zeus

This is a Zephyr book, first published in the UK in 2021
by Head of Zeus Ltd
This paperback edition first published in the UK in 2022
by Head of Zeus Ltd, part of Bloomsbury Publishing Plc

9 7 5 3 1 2 4 6 8

A catalogue record for this book is available from
the British Library.

ISBN (PB): 9781838935368
ISBN (E): 9781838935375

Typesetting and design
by Catherine Gaffney

Printed and bound in Serbia
by Publikum d.o.o.

Head of Zeus Ltd
5–8 Hardwick Street
London EC1R 4RG
WWW.HEADOFZEUS.COM

'Extinction is the rule. Survival is the exception.'

Carl Sagan

CONTENTS

Introduction   1

† What is Extinction?   5

? Why Do Species Go Extinct?   11

    ☀ Diseases, Predation and Competition   13

    🐝 Coextinction   17

    Genetic Mixing   19

    🌴 Habitat Destruction   20

    Climate Change   22

🕐 Timeline   24

☠ Mass Extinctions   27

🐘 The End Triassic Mass Extinction   33

    Causes   35

    Effects   45

🐗 Ask the Expert   54

🐗 Lisowicia   59

   🔍 *Lisowicia*: Discovery   60

   🦴 *Lisowicia*: Anatomy   66

   🧩 *Lisowicia*: Classification   73

   🐗 *Lisowicia*: Ecology   85

  Glossary   111

INTRODUCTION

For as long as there has been life on Earth, there has been extinction, and given enough time, all species will one day go extinct. Every day, it seems, we are hearing more and more tragic stories about increasing numbers of species moving closer to extinction. There are scientists, conservationists, charities, universities, communities and even a few good governments fighting against extinction and trying to save some of our most treasured species and habitats. But, and there is a *but* to this story, extinction has its place in our world and, at the right level and at the right time, it is a perfectly natural occurrence and can even help evolution in some ways.

I am a scientist. It's the very best job in the world. In my work, I look at evolution and I've been lucky enough to spend time with some of the most endangered species on our planet, as well as a few that have now gone extinct. I'm fascinated by the effects extinction has on nature, in the broader sense. But how much do we *really* know about the process of extinction?

If we are to ever stand a chance of saving species from extinction, then first we need to understand it. What is extinction? What causes it? What happens when many species go extinct at once? I want to explore extinction as a biological process and investigate why it can sometimes be a positive thing for evolution, as well as, at times, nature's most destructive force. Let's put it under the microscope and find out everything there is to know.

When a species is declared extinct, we place a dagger symbol (†) next to its name when it's listed or mentioned in a scientific manner. So, if you do see the name of a species with a little dagger after it, you'll know why. It's extinct. In this series, I have written about eight fantastic species. Starting with *Hallucigenia* (†), then *Dunkleosteus* (†) and trilobites (†), through to *Lisowicia* (†), *Tyrannosaurus rex* (†) and megalodon (†), before finishing with thylacine (†)

and lastly, the Hainan gibbon. Of these, only the Hainan gibbon does not have a dagger next to its scientific name, meaning it is the only animal we still have a chance of saving from extinction.

Professor Ben Garrod

WHAT IS EXTINCTION?

OFTEN, IN BIOLOGY, as is the case with much of science, there are many definitions for a lot of complicated terms. Understanding the essence of extinction, though, is not especially complicated – it is when a species is dead. Not just the individual animal or a large group of animals which are the same, but all animals of that species. When there are no more left alive and the last one dies, then that species is extinct. Lost. Gone forever.

Something I have a lot of trouble with when we talk about extinction is the question, 'So what? Who really cares if a species dies out? What difference does it make?

So what if another type of frog disappears?' The truth is there are people who you'll never convince that it's vitally important we fight against extinction right now. They're frequently the same people who don't believe our climate is rapidly changing, and who argue against so much of modern science. But why *does* it matter if a species disappears? There's a simple answer and a much more complex answer.

The simple answer is that as humans, we occupy a unique position in the animal kingdom. We understand a great deal. We have the power and the ability to completely shape and control the world around us, and with that comes a duty to protect others within our community, whether they're our human neighbours in our street or our animal neighbours in forests and reefs and in our gardens.

The second answer is because the natural world is a wondrous interconnected ecosystem, in which there are many examples of species linking to one another. Nature is like a big spider web, connecting billions of organisms with invisible strands. If one species is removed from that, it pulls on another part of the web. If enough species

are made extinct, then the whole structure
is destroyed. For example, sharks, tuna
and turtles all prey on jellyfish.
If all those predators are removed
from an ocean ecosystem,
jellyfish numbers shoot up
and suddenly there are so
many of them that they
are doing better than
small fish, like sardines.
The jellyfish eat so
much plankton that food
chains collapse and the
dangerous species of jellyfish
can sometimes make beaches unsafe
places for us. Because of the balance within
this global web of life, killing sharks can actually make
swimming in the sea more dangerous. With so many
species of plants, animals, fungi and other life, who
knows what catastrophic effect a species going extinct
might have.

Extinction has been present since the first life on Earth popped into existence, which must mean that loads *and loads* of species have gone extinct. It's hard to get your head around how many. Scientists predict that as many as 99 per cent of the species that have *ever* lived have gone extinct and if you're wondering how many species that might be, then if their calculations are correct, it means we have already lost an almost unbelievable five billion species from our planet.

We cannot be certain, because so many extinctions stretch back millions (or even hundreds of millions) of years and as there wasn't a scientist standing there with a camera or a notebook, we shall never know about many of these losses. Scientists believe that there may be 10–14 million different species (although some believe this figure might even be as high as one trillion). Of those, only 1.2 million have been documented and recorded in a proper scientific way, meaning we don't know about 90 per cent of life on planet Earth right now.

Here's where it gets a little complicated. Extinction is natural. Even we human beings will go extinct one day. It might sound sad, but that's because you're thinking from the point of view of a person. We are simply one of those 14 million or so species, remember. Usually, a species has about 10 million years or so of evolving, eating, chasing, playing, maybe doing homework, building nests or even going to the moon before it goes extinct and ends up in the history (or even prehistory) books. Some species last longer than this, some are around for less time.

WHY DO SPECIES GO EXTINCT?

IF I SAID to you there was going to be a terribly cold winter, you'd get a warm hat and coat ready. Or if I said there's a test coming, I'm hoping you'd do your revision and get an early night beforehand. That's because we naturally prepare for things, to increase our chances of succeeding. Nature is like that with species and extinction. The difference is that a species doesn't know it is heading into extinction (as far as we know, we are unique in that knowledge within the animal kingdom). Nevertheless, to some extent, a species prepares in the same way you might get ready for winter or an exam.

This might involve a physical change, such as the slight differences in the colour or pattern of some moths which help camouflage them better in a different environment. It might be a change in size or shape, like some island-living ancient relatives of elephants becoming smaller to cope with less food in their habitat. Sometimes the change is only seen at the genetic level, such as modern varieties of crops having better resistance to particular diseases; or it might even be a change in behaviour, such as peregrine falcons in cities hunting at night, rather than in the daytime, to catch their prey.

There are almost limitless reasons which might lead to extinction but they have one thing in common. They all focus on change. These changes can be either in the species' 'physical environment', such as the destruction of a habitat, through flooding or drought. Or it might be in its 'biological environment', such as the arrival of a new predator or the development of a new deadly disease. If the species does not have enough time to change or simply cannot change, then it will die out and become extinct. Let's look more closely at the variety of causes that can contribute directly or indirectly to the extinction of a species, or group of species.

DISEASES, PREDATION AND COMPETITION

Diseases are often linked to extinction. Practically every species alive has its own set of diseases and those which it can pick up from other species. It's easy to think of examples that cause massive problems, such as the famous 'Black Death' plague, but sometimes the most common and harmless condition can cause untold damage.

I was lucky enough to work with wild chimpanzees in Uganda. I lived in a forest and spent every day following the chimps to study them. I also took tourists out in a responsible way, so that the chimps and their habitat would be protected from hunters and habitat destruction.

To keep the chimps safe, we always kept a distance between us and them. Because they are our closest living relatives, we share almost every branch on the evolutionary tree, meaning we are similar in many ways. It also means that we can share many of the same diseases. Among them is the common cold, something that has evolved with us in the five million years or so since we split from a common ancestor with chimps. For us, a cold means having the sniffles and a runny nose for a few days. When a chimpanzee catches our cold, though, it can be deadly, and in 2018, scientists found that wild chimps at a famous tourist site in Uganda died after catching a cold. All it would have taken was for a tourist with the sniffles to get too close and sadly, that was it.

In a natural situation, it's unusual for a predator to cause the total extinction of its prey, because the two are in balance, where both evolve to be better predators, or better at avoiding predators. This delicate relationship takes millions of years to develop and is a good example of what we call coevolution, where the evolution of two species is closely tied together. But when a predator is suddenly introduced to an environment, the prey has no time to evolve sufficiently to avoid being eaten.

When Australian farmers had problems with native beetles eating their sugar cane crop, the Bureau of Sugar Experiment Stations decided to bring in a predator which could eat the hard-shelled beetles and their hidden larvae. So in 1935, they introduced cane toads from Hawaii. The bad news was that the cane toads did not seem to go for the beetles they were *supposed* to eat, and the really bad news was that they seemed to prefer eating everything else instead and they now hunt many species of native invertebrates, fish, amphibians, reptiles, birds and mammals. Only 102 baby toads were originally released, but it is thought there are now more than 200 million of them and that they represent not only a major source of predation but also an ecological disaster for the whole Australian ecosystem.

It's tough enough for any species – dealing with predators, harsh environments and the daily struggle between life and death. It gets even worse when you have to compete with other species for food or somewhere to live. Competition is either natural, such as leopards, lions and hyenas competing for food on the savannas of East Africa, or can be caused by humans – for example, overfishing in our oceans means less food for sharks.

The Labrador duck was, we think, always rare along the eastern coastline of North America and Canada where it lived, but after European settlers arrived, its fate was sadly sealed. Most extinctions have more than one cause and this seems to have been the case with these small brown, black and white ducks. They were hunted, but not as much as other ducks were because, apparently, they tasted pretty bad. That's at least one way to avoid predators. But it seems as though competition

may also have played a part in their extinction. Labrador ducks ate mussels and other shellfish in the shallow waters along the coastline, but as the human population grew, they, too, ate the local shellfish and, as you might expect, they took much more than the ducks. Because the Labrador ducks could never compete with humans, there was less and less food for them, and their population continued to fall. The last living Labrador duck was seen in 1878 and the species was then declared extinct.

COEXTINCTION

Sometimes a species evolves alongside another species so closely that when one goes extinct, there is nothing the other can do but go extinct too. This might be a specific parasite depending on a specific host species or maybe a particular pollinating insect needing one species of plant in order to survive.

An extreme example of a coextinction is the moa and the Haast's eagle. Moa were huge flightless birds found on New Zealand, with some being as much as 3.6m in height and 230kg in weight. The Haast's eagle was their main

When the large flightless moa was hunted to extinction by humans on New Zealand's South Island, it also meant the end for the Haast's eagle.

predator. When human settlers hunted the last moa into extinction around 600 years ago, the eagles were left with no food and they, too, went extinct.

GENETIC MIXING

Every species has its own set of unique genetic data. It's like the species' recipe. If a little bit of it is changed, then it's a different species, just like a recipe. Sometimes recipes are similar, like chocolate cake and chocolate fudge cake, and other times they're very different, such as chocolate cake and cheese on toast. In the same way, some species are more closely related to one another than to others. When this happens, there is a chance they may breed and produce what we call hybrids. When this happens, there is a real risk that one (or even both) of the original species could eventually go extinct, with the combined mixture being their offspring. There is nothing wrong with this, but it does change that original species 'recipe'.

Wild boar and domestic (farmyard) pigs are similar but there are differences. Some scientists believe they are completely separate species, but others say they are more closely related and are what we call two subspecies. However much they differ, one thing which is certain is that they are able to breed with each another. In the UK, there are populations of wild boar living close to pig farms. When pigs have escaped or been released from these farms, they have bred with their wild cousins and the offspring have been hybrids of pigs and boar. If this happens over and over again, it might mean that eventually, the original recipe of wild boar is changed and the species may no longer exist.

HABITAT DESTRUCTION 🌴

When we talk about this cause of extinction, we usually use the phrase 'habitat loss' but, to be blunt, we don't *lose* habitats, we *destroy* them. Admitting what we actually do is a big step in the right direction needed to protect many habitats and ecosystems around the world. The saddest thing about habitat destruction is that it means devastation, not just for many individual organisms but sometimes for entire species too.

I read about an amazing discovery. A friend of mine was part of a team which announced *today* (as in, the day I wrote this) they had scientifically described a brand-new species of monkey, which they have called the Popa langur. These funky-looking, grey-haired, wide-eyed monkeys are found in the Southeast Asian country of Myanmar. To find a new species is a lifelong dream for many biologists and a cause for celebration. But even though there is a lot to celebrate about this new discovery, there's bad news as well. There are no more than 260 of these monkeys left and already they are classified as being Critically Endangered. Their forest homes are disappearing because they are being illegally cut down for timber or being cleared for farming, and nearby cities and towns are growing larger all the time. This is the newest species we know about but it's already only a step away from being lost forever, all because we have destroyed its forest home.

CLIMATE CHANGE

Some big things happen really quickly, such as a bolt of lightning or an earthquake. Others take time, but have an impact that is as big, or even bigger. The biggest of these threats is climate change. Right now, it sits above mudslides and avalanches, tsunamis and forest fires. It's easy to imagine that any of these natural disasters is a terrible threat, and they are. But whereas an avalanche might kill hundreds of animals, a tsunami might mean the end of thousands of animals and forest fires might take millions of lives, the true effects of climate change on our planet are hard to imagine. Trillions and trillions of animals, plants and other organisms are at risk, meaning millions of species will be pushed into extinction.

As our world grows warmer, our seas become more acidic and ocean levels rise, and the need to act has never been greater. It's easy to find species which have already *gone* extinct due to climate change. Everything from the mighty *Tyrannosaurus rex* to the sabre-toothed cat have been lost to climate change. What's even easier is to predict which species are *going* to be in trouble because of climate change. The answer is simple. It's most of them. Unless we act now.

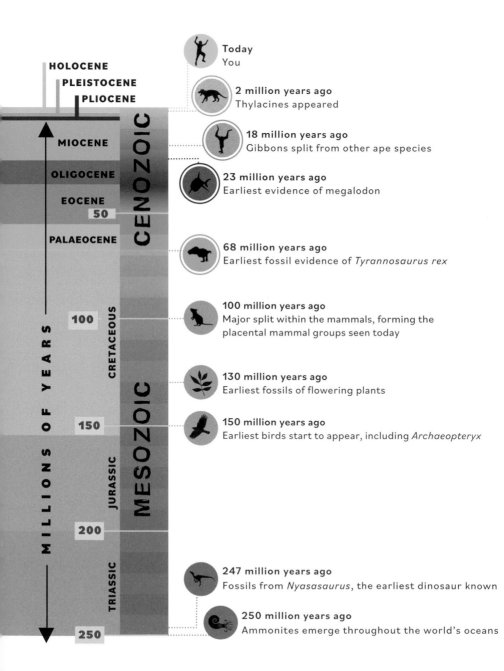

HOLOCENE
PLEISTOCENE
PLIOCENE

MIOCENE

OLIGOCENE

EOCENE
50

PALAEOCENE

CENOZOIC

100

CRETACEOUS

150

MESOZOIC

JURASSIC

200

TRIASSIC

250

MILLIONS OF YEARS

Today
You

2 million years ago
Thylacines appeared

18 million years ago
Gibbons split from other ape species

23 million years ago
Earliest evidence of megalodon

68 million years ago
Earliest fossil evidence of *Tyrannosaurus rex*

100 million years ago
Major split within the mammals, forming the placental mammal groups seen today

130 million years ago
Earliest fossils of flowering plants

150 million years ago
Earliest birds start to appear, including *Archaeopteryx*

247 million years ago
Fossils from *Nyasasaurus*, the earliest dinosaur known

250 million years ago
Ammonites emerge throughout the world's oceans

MILLIONS OF YEARS

PALAEOZOIC

PERMIAN

300

CARBONIFEROUS

350

DEVONIAN

400

SILURIAN

ORDOVICIAN

450

CAMBRIAN

500

PROTEROZOIC

ARCHEAN

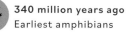

300 million years ago
Lisowicia first appeared

320 million years ago
'Mammal-like reptiles', including *Dimetrodon*, evolve

340 million years ago
Earliest amphibians

382 million years ago
Earliest evidence of *Dunkleosteus*

385 million years ago
Oldest fossilised tree

400 million years ago
Earliest fossils of insects

Some of the dates for earliest fossils are estimates based on our best understanding right now. They are not always perfect and the more evidence we collect, the more certain we can be and the more accurate these dates will eventually become.

500 million years ago
Fossil evidence from *Hallucigenia*

520 million years ago
Earliest vertebrates emerged (and may have looked like small eels)

530 million years ago
Earliest fossils of trilobites

680 million years ago
Earliest ancestors of jellyfish and their relatives

2.15 billion years ago
Earliest evidence of bacteria

3 billion years ago
Earliest evidence of viruses

MASS EXTINCTIONS

RIGHT NOW, somewhere in the world, something, for some reason will be going extinct, hopefully due to natural causes. In the same way that the evolution and appearance of a species is completely natural, so too is the constant loss of species. Species come and go in a cycle, a bit like tides moving back and forth or the changing of the seasons.

Extinction is unavoidable and goes on at a fairly predictable rate wherever life exists. We call this background extinction: constant, low-level extinction which doesn't cause major problems on a wider scale, other than for

Hallucigenia

the species going extinct, that is. These 'every day extinctions' go mostly unnoticed by the majority of us. This all changes when we are talking about a mass extinction. For the purposes of my books, we are going to treat a mass extinction as the worldwide loss of around 75 per cent (or more) of species, over a short space of 'geological' time. If you're wondering how short 'a short space of geological time' is, then let's say it has to be under three million years. This might sound a very long time, but remember Earth is around four and a half *billion* years old. By making our timeframe three million years we catch the sudden disastrous mass extinctions, such as the dinosaur-killing asteroid End Cretaceous event, as well as some of the mass extinctions which played out over hundreds of thousands or even millions of years ago.

Dunkleosteus

Trilobite

Mass extinctions, as you might expect, involve loss of life on an enormous scale, either across a large number of species or groups, or across a significant part of the planet, or both. In a mass extinction event, the rate of species being lost is greater than the rate by which species are evolving. Imagine you're slowly filling a bucket with water, but there's a big hole in its side; over time, the bucket will still become empty.

Over the last 500 million years or so, the Earth has experienced multiple mass extinctions, ranging from five to as many as 20 depending on what definitions (and there are a number of different ones) scientists use. In the worst of these mass extinction events, over 90 per cent of life on Earth has been wiped out, and in terms of life recovering to a level from before the event, it may take at least 10 million years for biodiversity levels to return

Tyrannosaurus rex

to what they were. Some mass extinctions, like the one caused by the asteroid 66 million years ago at the end of the Cretaceous period, are pretty quick, while others spread across hundreds of thousands of years to take full effect.

Megalodon

When we talk about mass extinctions, most scientists agree there are five classic mass extinctions, with the earliest occurring around 450 million years ago and the most recent 66 million years ago. In addition to these famous five mass extinctions, another has been identified recently, which struck around 2.5 million years ago.

Now, many scientists say we are entering (or even in) the sixth mass extinction event, but this is something

Thylacine

which needs to be looked at closely for two reasons. First, I've just mentioned the recently identified mass extinction which occurred just over two million years ago, which would make that the sixth mass extinction, so the current global extinction event would be the seventh, in fact. Second, as we'll see later in the series, it's really hard to say exactly when most mass extinctions start, so, as bad as it is right now, we may not even be in one yet.

Hainan gibbon

Throughout the series, we're going to look at the five classic mass extinctions, the newly discovered mass extinction and the current extinction event which is being triggered by us. Finally, we'll look at how scientists and conservationists are tackling the threat of extinction now and explore what can be done.

THE END TRIASSIC MASS EXTINCTION

SOME MASS EXTINCTIONS are just too spectacular to imagine and sound as though they were conjured by the imagination of an excitable action film crew. I cannot begin to understand what worldwide blooms of life-choking green algae in the oceans caused by trees on land at the end of the Devonian looked like. Or how it was possible to survive the global devastation caused by a huge asteroid travelling tens of thousands of kilometres an hour, then smashing into the shallow seas off Mexico before changing the climate across the Earth and killing off the mighty dinosaurs.

Other mass extinctions are easier to picture and, in many ways, are scarier than the 'big' ones. The End Triassic mass extinction is just such an episode. Although the causes are different, the effects on the planet and the life inhabiting it are worryingly similar to what we are seeing now. Of all the mass extinctions the Earth has encountered, this is the one we can learn the most from. If we ignore the changes we need to implement now, then what happened at the end of the Triassic might give us a glimpse of what's to come!

After the previous mass extinction ended the Permian (per-ME an) period around 252.2 million years ago, the Earth entered the Triassic (TRY-ass-ik) period. That last extinction event, known also as the 'Great Dying', was intense, changing the planet so much that we don't just mark this point as ending a period of time but as a point at which a new era started. This is a much bigger division and is like comparing months to years or decades to centuries. At the end of the Permian, life changed so drastically that it ended the Palaeozoic (PAY-LEE-O zo-ik) era and saw the start of the Mesozoic (mez-O zo-ik) era, which would become famous for being the block of time where dinosaurs dominated the planet. The Mesozoic was broken into three smaller periods, and the Triassic was the first and shortest of these, lasting 50.6 million years. The period finished with the End Triassic mass extinction event around 201.3 million years ago.

CAUSES 🌡️❄️

A possible cause of the End Triassic mass extinction might have been a large asteroid strike, similar to the one we later see at the end of the Cretaceous period. It's a great idea and would explain everything nicely, but the only problem is that we don't really have evidence for such a strike. There is, though, a large circular site in Portugal, which stretches for 35km. When scientists estimated the age of this impact crater, they discovered it dates back about 200 million years, to around the time of the mass extinction. Although tantalising, it is most likely a coincidence, because so far, scientists haven't been able to link this impact with the extinction itself.

There has also been some research which identified a crater site in Quebec, Canada, as a possible culprit. Here, there is a series of lakes, almost 100km across, called the Manicouagan crater. If you look this up online, you'll be amazed – it looks like just the sort of thing that could have been responsible for wiping out most of life on Earth. More research has been carried out that shows it was

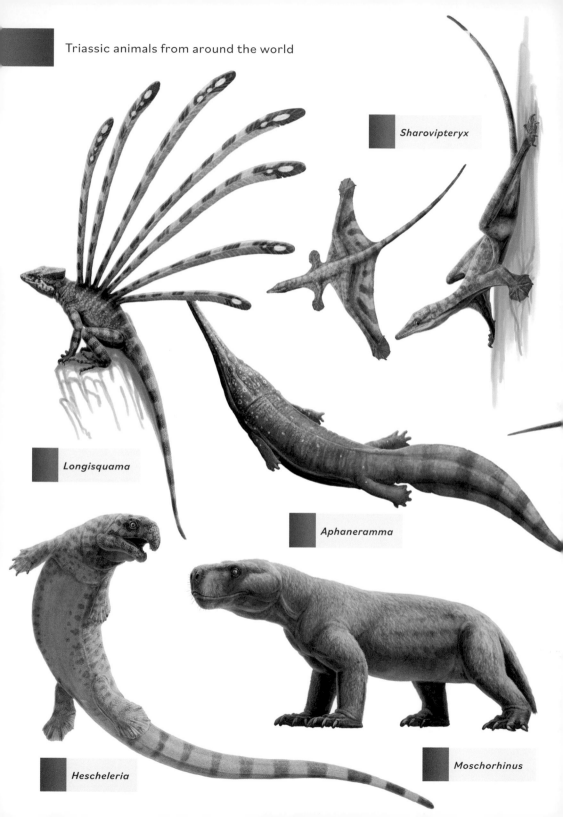

Triassic animals from around the world

Sharovipteryx

Longisquama

Aphaneramma

Hescheleria

Moschorhinus

Tanystropheus

Drepanosaurus

Nicrosaurus

Garjainia

Shringasaurus

indeed caused by an asteroid similar in size to that which, millions of years later, wiped out *Tyrannosaurus rex* and her buddies. However, this one seems to have caused no widespread damage, other than for the unlucky individuals underneath and in the immediate area, and it struck 14 million years before the mass extinction actually started. It does seem with mass extinctions that we often start off by saying 'OK, let's look for evidence of an asteroid and then we can look for other causes'. Until more evidence of an asteroid is uncovered, either reinforcing this extra-terrestrial theory or completely disproving it, we need to look at other possible causes, and there is a lot of evidence which supports a different scenario.

Luckily, there is another prime suspect in terms of what caused the End Triassic mass extinction and this one definitely left clues, over a wide section of the planet. When we're young and see an image or a piece of film of a volcano erupting, we realise how deadly the lava is, how it would incinerate everything in its path as it flows across the land and showers into the air. I remember thinking that volcanoes could end the world, but I learned that the impact of an eruption is local and that it is people, wildlife

and places nearby that are in danger. But
then I discovered that this isn't always true
and that yes, sometimes volcanoes *do* end worlds after
all. They can be so powerful and devastating that they
affect all life on Earth and change the planet.

Earth's crust and the layer just below it form a
gigantic, globe-shaped, 3D jigsaw of seven or eight
massive pieces, or tectonic (tek ton-ik) plates, and many
smaller plates. These plates sit on a layer of mostly solid
rock in the thick layer which makes up the mantle. The
strength of the mantle is different to the strength of the
layer making up the tectonic plates and this allows them
to slowly slide against each another. This, in turn, means
that some plates grow larger and some grow smaller, as
they push against neighbouring plates or move away from
one another. This is the quickest and simplest overview
of plate tectonics ever, but it's an overview you need in
order to understand what happened at the end of the
Triassic period.

At the places where the plates meet, there is a lot of
activity and energy, as some plate edges are pushed down
into the Earth and others increase their area and need to fill

in the gaps along their newly forming edges. Most of us never feel the effects of this, but it's happening now, thousands of kilometres beneath our feet. While some plates don't really move at all, others move by as much as 10cm every year. We are, at the moment, in a fairly calm period in terms of our planet's tectonic activity, but around 200 million years ago, things were about to change drastically. And not in a good way. For about 30 million years the supercontinent Pangaea (pan JEE-a) had been in the process of breaking up into newer supercontinents and some of the smaller continents we'd one day recognise as being home. This hadn't caused many problems, but then something went wrong.

Evidence of a vast amount of volcanic activity at the end of the Triassic period can now be seen across a huge area of our modern-day planet. Look at New York and as far west as Texas, as far south as Venezuela and Brazil and as far east as France and the Atlas Mountains of Morocco, and you'll see great walls of cooled lava and other rock formations caused by this same event. The evidence of the End Triassic volcanic activity today covers an area of more than six million square kilometres of the planet, on either side of the Atlantic Ocean. In fact, it's this body of water which is in many ways to blame for what happened just over 200 million years ago. As Pangaea continued on its journey of breaking up, a section separated and created an ocean, the Atlantic. It formed along a line where two major tectonic plates met and over time, it separated further and further and eventually filled with water and created the ocean we know today. But at the end of the Triassic, this line, where these two great plates met, ran from where New York is today down to Brazil, and the reason it is also seen in France, Morocco and Venezuela is because before the Atlantic formed, these places were next to each other, in a line running from north to south.

Then, 201.6 million years ago, a series of volcanic eruptions, lava fields and giant geysers created a world-changing episode. Scientists call this area of devastation the Central Atlantic Magmatic Province (or 'CAMP' for short). Overall, the CAMP was active for between 500,000 and 600,000 years over four periods of intense waves of destruction. If you, by any chance, are a time-travelling geology tourist and thinking about going back to see what the CAMP would have looked like up close, it's probably a place you're best off avoiding. There would have been fountains of molten liquid rock gushing over a kilometre high and landscapes filled with lava lakes, underground

Nothing could have survived within the Central Atlantic Magmatic Province (CAMP) landscape and, because it remained active for over half a million years, it devastated life across the planet.

rivers of magma, and chains hundreds of kilometres long of violently active volcanoes. Some individual volcanic eruptions may have lasted for as long as 100,000 years. Although the eruptions covered a period of more than half a million years, it was during just one of the four waves of destruction which marks the CAMP that most of the extinctions took place. In this 20,000-year window around 75 per cent of the life on our planet went extinct.

If you are still tempted to go back and see what the CAMP eruptions were like, you might think you'd be safe if you were far away and looked through binoculars or even a telescope. In a way, you'd be right. For any life in the immediate area, deadly lava from the CAMP meant instant death, but lava didn't kill everything. What you may not know is that even if you were thousands of kilometres away from the nearest volcano, you'd still be in trouble. That number of volcanoes and such a high a level of volcanic activity meant that phenomenal levels of volcanic gases were released into the atmosphere, signifying certain death for much of life on Earth.

EFFECTS

It's a story we hear again and again when we look at the mass extinctions which scar the history of life on Earth. Something dreadful happened which, at first glance, might explain why so much died out, but then it's what happened next that was responsible for the ecological mayhem. The End Triassic mass extinction is similar because all that lava and fire seems to explain what happened to those species lost, but actually it was the gases the volcanic activity released that we're interested in. As with other mass extinctions, it was the changes in gases within the environment that did the lasting damage in the End Triassic mass extinction.

Any volcanic eruption gives out a range of different gases. Some are instantly toxic, some have a cooling effect and others have a warming effect. The one we're probably most familiar with is carbon dioxide. Now, on its own, carbon dioxide isn't a problem. It's all around you – every time you breathe in, some carbon dioxide goes into your body and every time you breathe out, a little bit more leaves your body. But if there is too much, that's when the problems start.

When we look at the environment, carbon dioxide has one of two main impacts (and sometimes both). First, it warms the planet, and of the two impacts, this is the easier one to understand. When there is suddenly a load more carbon dioxide, it prevents the heat from the sun, which has hit the Earth, from radiating back out into space and escaping out of the atmosphere. If you have ever done any gardening, then you'll have seen the same effect inside a greenhouse, but instead of gas preventing the heat from escaping, it's the panes of glass. This is why we call the problems with gases causing the planet to warm the 'greenhouse effect'. Increasing the temperature like this causes polar habitats to melt, desert ecosystems to spread and wetlands to dry out. It affects everything, from when different species can breed to which plants can grow in an area.

We can see this in the fossilised plants from the end of the Triassic period. Leaves take in carbon dioxide from the atmosphere through lots of little specialised holes on the leaves themselves. Usually, plants will have lots of these pores but if the levels of carbon dioxide in the air suddenly go up, then after a while, plants evolve to need fewer of these holes.

When scientists look at the number of pores from fossil leaves at the end of the Triassic, they found far fewer holes than they'd expected, meaning there was a *lot* of carbon dioxide in our atmosphere. Levels of this extinction-causing gas may have as much as tripled in a fairly short period of time.

Increasing carbon dioxide levels also cause a major issue in the oceans and other marine ecosystems. Carbon dioxide is absorbed by seawater, and the more there is, the more is absorbed. When these two react, they form an acid, called carbonic acid, which, over time, increases the acidity of the seawater itself. If the acidity increases, it can destroy large parts of a marine ecosystem by killing small organisms that have either soft external skeletons or shells that are destroyed by the acid.

If you need an example, then here's an easy but powerful experiment you can do. You'll need a stick of white chalk, three glasses, water and some household vinegar. In our experiment, the chalk represents coral reefs. They are both made from calcium carbonate, even if they don't look very similar. Vinegar is a very weak acid and can be used to show what happened (and is happening) in oceans across the planet.

Break the chalk into three similar-sized pieces and place one in each glass. Half-fill the first glass with water and add a teaspoon of vinegar. Fill the second glass with roughly the same amount of water but this time add more vinegar. To be more scientifically accurate, three or four teaspoons will do, but if you want faster and more dramatic results, then add 10 spoonfuls. In the third, do the same again but this time place the glass somewhere warm – on a sunny windowsill or next to a heater or radiator if you live somewhere cooler. Then watch.

Nothing should happen to the first glass, but the chalk in glasses two and three should start fizzing (depending on how much vinegar you added). This is because the acid is dissolving the calcium carbonate. This isn't a massive problem for a piece of chalk but means death for a coral, which has a body framework made from the same stuff, and it's catastrophic for coral reefs as ecosystems.

Depending on how warm the water is, the chalk in the third glass should dissolve even faster, showing that in warmer oceans higher levels of ocean acidification spell

disaster for marine ecosystems past, present and future. After a day or so, the chalk in your acidic glasses will have dissolved completely. It's not too difficult to imagine what this process does to a real coral reef.

When we look at the End Triassic mass extinction, the evidence shows that among the most devastating effects was the impact it had on the world's coral reefs. Corals had flourished throughout the Triassic and then spread and diversified, so that reefs became widespread and important habitats. This mass extinction almost entirely wiped them out. Few survived and as a type of ecosystem and habitat, that was very nearly it for coral reefs.

Triassic biodiversity was dazzling, with both terrestrial and marine habitats full of life. An *Atopodentatus*, a herbivorous marine reptile with a hammer-shaped head, feeds on a tropical reef during the Middle Triassic, in what is now China.

It took almost 300,000 years for corals and coral reefs to return, leaving a big gap in the fossil record. This drastic decline in the numbers and diversity of corals and the widespread loss of reefs is eerily similar to what we are seeing today. Although the End Triassic mass extinction is responsible for the most significant loss of corals and reefs so far, we may be heading into a similar situation – or one which might even be worse because of the way we are treating our planet.

Within ocean ecosystems, groups of animals went extinct and roughly a third of all groups of marine organisms were lost. On land, many groups went extinct and many representatives from other groups were lost, meaning extinctions were widespread. Groups such as the heavily armoured herbivorous aetosaurs (AY-tow sors) and the terrifying, huge rauisuchians (raw-EE suke-EE-ans), which looked like a cross between crocodiles and predatory dinosaurs, both went extinct. Others had a lucky escape and many

Poposaurus - a poposauroid

Desmatosuchus – an aetosaur

plants, mammals, pterosaurs and the dinosaurs survived largely unaffected, although many species within these groups still went extinct.

Overall, some scientists believe that as much as 40 per cent of the land vertebrates were lost in this mass extinction, including many of the animals known as 'proto-mammals'. These early ancestors and relatives of ours are sometimes called the 'mammal-like reptiles' but this is not a good name, partly because they're not reptiles! Members of the group would later evolve into mammals, but during the Triassic, this was a group of many strange and wonderful animals, including *Lisowicia* (liz-O wik-EE-a). As with any mass extinction, if there are winners, there have to be losers, and along with so many others, *Lisowicia* was among the unfortunate losers.

Postosuchus – a rauisuchian

Dr Jessica H. Whiteside is an associate professor at the University of Southampton. She is a palaeo-climate scientist and palaeontologist studying fossilised molecular clues of how events like gigantic volcanic eruptions and meteorites smashing into Earth lead to mass extinction events.

What can past climate change teach us about modern-day species loss?

Amazingly enough, for over 3.5 billion years, life on Earth has blossomed, exploded and diversified from tiny single-celled bacteria invisible to the naked eye, to huge blue whales that weigh as much as 30 *Tyrannosaurus rex* dinosaurs! All life forms are tenacious go-getters, expanding into each and every ecosystem on our planet.

Extinctions of whole species also occur, and expansion and extinction together make up a natural evolutionary see-saw that is often in balance. But when the loss of species becomes much greater than the creation of new species in a short amount of time, the see-saw can be tipped enough to cause a so-called 'mass extinction'. Given the vast amount of time since life first evolved on the planet, 'short' can be anything from hundreds of thousands of years to a couple of million.

There have been at least five epic extinction events when the see-saw tipped. Perhaps the most famous was 66 million years ago, when a large space rock hanging about in our Milky Way fell out of orbit and collided into southern Mexico. It set off a series of environmental chain reactions like a game of deadly dominoes.

- Debris from the impact blew into the atmosphere, circled the Earth and then rained back down, heating the air to hotter than your barbecue.
- Rock-vaporising impact caused a sooty dust cloud that blocked the sun and stopped photosynthesis.
- Greenhouse gases in the oceans caused acidification. This ate away the mineralised covering that makes the shells of sea creatures, in much the same way as an invasive cavity damages your teeth.
- An unimaginable alternation of heat and freeze took place in a matter of hundreds of years.

Ultimately, these environmental changes were too drastic and happened too fast for large organisms to adjust or adapt. The result was that *T. rex* and the other non-flying dinosaurs (as well as many marine creatures, like giant plesiosaur reptiles and the coiled ammonites) bit the dust. That paved the way for better-adapted burrowing mammals, no larger than hedgehogs, to take the stage and eventually lead to us. Yes, the see-saw tipped.

Events other than meteorite impacts can also cause mass extinctions. Some 135 million years earlier, at the end of the Triassic, the eruption of gigantic fissure volcanoes and outpourings of colossal curtains of lava covered an area a third as big as our moon. These events caused a climate catastrophe and a mass extinction that led to the rise of dinosaurs at the expense of fierce, but waddling, crocodile-like creatures. There was no place to run and hide anymore.

Even earlier in Earth's history, at the end of the Permian, similar-sized eruptions and climate change triggered what is possibly the largest great dying event of all time. Ninety per cent of all animals went extinct, leaving a few survivors known as 'disaster-species' to inherit the Earth. Imagine that during your last walk through the forest, you close your eyes and open them again to see only one of every ten things still remaining. Goosebumps, indeed.

Why should we study these past events of doom and gloom? We look to our past for lessons in understanding the natural progression of the building up of diversity, and of its destruction. These past episodes highlight the dramatic and lasting implications of climate change to species – extinction.

By many accounts, we are in the middle of a mass extinction, but fortunately not all is lost. As guardians of the geological and fossil record, we can use past extinctions to extract possible solutions that can help us to help reduce the risk. For example, we can attempt to mimic natural ways of pulling greenhouse gases out of our atmosphere, lessening their warming effects. And we can advise on ways to save vulnerable species, including our own.

LISOWICIA

ONE OF the very best things about science (and there are *lots* of very cool things about science and being a scientist) is the element of surprise. When most of us imagine 'impressive' animals, we tend to think of predators. I have no idea why that should be, but it seems that a meat-eater in the natural world is somehow considered superior. In fact, some of the largest, most intelligent and most aggressive members of the animal kingdom aren't carnivores – think about blue whales, chimpanzees and hippopotamuses as three examples of being huge, brainy or just really fearsome.

Then there's the idea that we know everything there is to know in this world. You'd be amazed at how often I hear people say that. Luckily, they're wrong, because there is still so much more to learn about nature and the wider world around us. An animal like *Lisowicia* fits into both these categories, as it was an example of a herbivore which was both huge and fearsome-looking, *and* it was only recently discovered. The discovery of *Lisowicia* was a big part of the puzzle needed to help us understand a period of time over 200 million years ago, when the planet was still very different to the one we know today. I wonder how many more immense and exciting discoveries are out there, waiting to be found.

DISCOVERY 🔍

Sometimes, when a new species (whether it's extinct or still alive) is discovered or scientifically described, it is named after a person. The Devonian superpredator *Dunkleosteus* was named after David Dunkle, who was a curator of a natural history museum near to where some of the famous fish fossils were found. Sometimes, a species is given a name which helps describe the organism itself, such as *Tyrannosaurus rex*, meaning 'tyrant lizard king', which may not be the most accurate description ever, but does give you an idea of how impressive the 19th-century palaeontologists thought this predator was. Other species are named after places, such as the lone star tick, which has the name *Amblyomma americanum* (am-BLEE-O-ma am-er-ik-arn-um), because it's found across the USA, and a bizarre flower found in Borneo is called *Rafflesia borneensis* (raf-fl-EEZ-ya born-E-en-sis). Despite having no stems, leaves or roots, this is one of the largest flowers in the world and smells like a rotting animal to attract flies, which then pollinate it.

In a similar fashion, *Lisowicia* was named after the place where the first fossils were found. In southern Poland, there is a village called Lisowice and it's there, in a clay pit, that *Lisowicia* was discovered in 2006. But like any good mystery story, there's a twist. When Dr Grzegorz Niedźwiedzki and professors Tomasz Sulej and Jerzy Dzik originally discovered, removed and safely stored the fossils for further study, they understandably thought they were the bones from one of the earliest relatives from a group which would later form the giant sauropod dinosaurs, such as *Diplodocus*, *Patagotitan* and *Dreadnoughtus*. These proto-sauropods were called sauropodamorpha (sor-O PODE-a mor-fa) and were only starting to form during

the late Triassic. Many of them remain undiscovered and undescribed by scientists, so it makes sense that a bunch of huge bones dating from a time when the only big things on land were the sauropodamorphs would be seen as belonging to that group.

It was only in 2008 that the team realised the fossilised bones belonged to a totally different type of animal, from a group which had never been found in Europe and, in places where they were found, were usually much, much smaller. The team realised that the bones were from a giant animal in the group called the dicynodonts (DI SI-NO donts).

Until this point, although lots of Triassic dicynodont fossils had been found across Africa, Asia, North America and South America, only one or two bones had ever been found in Europe, making this discovery the most significant find for the region. Over the next six years, the team continued their exploration and found more than 1,000 bones from two sets of *Lisowicia* fossils in the pits. It was not until early 2019 that the scientists were finally ready to present their detailed findings and newly named discovery to the world, making it one of the most important, and most recent, Triassic fossil discoveries on the planet.

Dicynodonts were found around the world, in all shapes and sizes. In early Triassic Antarctica, a large dicynodont (*Lystrosaurus maccaigi*) meets another group (*Lystrosaurus curvatus*). Two smaller dicynodonts (*Myosaurus gracilis*) watch from the safety of the rocks.

ANATOMY

What's really big, has four legs, eats plants and lived tens of millions of years ago? Well, it's not mammoths, they were too recent. It can only really be the big dinosaurs. Animals such as *Patagotitan*, *Diplodocus* or the smaller 'big' ones such as *Triceratops* maybe. For a long time, the only early prehistoric giants we knew about were the dinosaurs, and the earliest dinosaur giants were the big-bodied, long-necked sauropods and their relatives. Yet the discovery of *Lisowicia* upset everything we thought we knew about the earliest land giants on our planet. Although animals did get much, much larger as time went on, this was one of the largest animals of the Triassic.

It was also the largest member of the group called synapsids (and there's a lot more about those in the Classification section of this chapter) for hundreds of millions of years, until large mammals started forming around 40 million years ago.

Although we don't have all the bones, it is possible to estimate how much *Lisowicia* weighed. This is notoriously difficult with extinct animals, because we can't just weigh them as we can an elephant or hippo. The skin and muscle have gone, the skeletons are often incomplete and the bones themselves have literally turned into rock. A method

which is used to estimate the weight and body mass of the sauropod dinosaurs is to measure the circumference of the largest bone (the humerus) in the forelimb and the largest bone (the femur) in the hindlimb. Once you have these, it's possible to apply a mathematical formula which estimates the total mass of the animal. When this was first done with *Lisowicia*, scientists concluded it would have been 4.5m long and weighed 9.3 tonnes (which is almost twice as much as the biggest African elephants today). But science never stands still, new techniques are developed and different teams find different results.

4.5m

Territorial *Lisowicia* displayed to one another to show how large and powerful they were. Weighing twice as much as an elephant, these were formidable and dangerous animals.

This has happened with *Lisowicia*, when researchers noticed that the bones measured were much thicker and larger than you might expect for an animal this size, meaning the original weight estimates were too high. When the weirdly thick bones were taken into consideration, the more realistic results estimated that it would have weighed around 5.9 tonnes. Even at this lower weight, *Lisowicia* was still the largest land animal which wasn't a dinosaur alive during the Triassic.

The position of the bones in the legs was also important. *Lisowicia* had upright limbs, which were positioned horizontally to the ground and specially adapted for moving at either walking pace or something a little faster. It's possible that, like a modern-day rhino or hippo, *Lisowicia* may have been able to move quickly for short periods, when necessary. It had a short tail, short neck and a large, solid skull. The skull had a long ridge at the back which allowed large muscles to stretch from there to the jaw, meaning *Lisowicia* had a powerful bite. It had no teeth but a tortoise-like beak at the front of the skull. It did not have the two big tusks found on many of

the animals in the group to which *Lisowicia* belonged, but it did have two large triangular bony plates on either side of the beak.

The bones in the neck of *Lisowicia* housed a strange secret. The vertebrae have hollow pits in their sides, similar to the holes found in the same bones in sauropods. In these dinosaurs, these holes are part of their respiratory system and helped them breathe, but they are different enough from the hole-filled vertebrae seen in sauropods to make it unclear what role they played for *Lisowicia*.

When we look at *Lisowicia*'s skeleton, we see that its bones grew differently to those of many animals we're more familiar with. We have a lot of growing to do when we are very young but this slows down and then stops when we're between 18 and 21 years old. *Lisowicia* was different because the fossils do not show that the bones stopped growing when the animal was an adult. In a similar way that tree rings can be used to look at their growth rates, bones can show the same. Scientists believe that *Lisowicia* grew quickly when it was young and continued growing throughout its life. Rapid growth would have been ideal for allowing young *Lisowicia* to reach a size where they would have become safe from predators. The ability to grow continuously meant that if the environment was good and food was available, the animal could have become bigger and bigger, which may have also helped it secure larger territories or attract a mate.

CLASSIFICATION

How do you know the difference between one species and another? There are lots of ways, but as you'll see, there are problems with many of these ways, too. The name is a good place to start, obviously. We all recognise different organisms by the names we give them. The difficulty with this is that names don't always translate that well, either in different languages or even in different parts of the world.

For many shark-lovers, their favourite is the great white. It's easily one of the most iconic and recognisable animals on the planet. But for me, it's the zebra shark.

They look cool, they're a weird shape and they are the most chilled-out animal on the reef. They're known as zebra sharks, even though the adults don't have stripes. Nearly everywhere in the world, people call them zebra sharks, apart from in Australia, where they are known as leopard sharks. And this is even more confusing when you realise there's another species called the leopard shark, which looks completely different.

And if you're maybe thinking that I should have chosen the great white after all and avoided the confusion, then even the most famous member of the shark family suffers from occasional mistaken identity and is also known as the white shark, white pointer and even by the gruesome name 'the white death'.

This is why we give every species on the planet, regardless of whether it's alive or extinct, a scientific name, to help us identify the species wherever you are on the planet or whichever language you speak. The

Stegostoma fasciatum

Triakis semifasciata

zebra shark
has the scientific name
Stegostoma fasciatum, for example. Each
scientific name is always written in italics and is made up
of two parts. The first part is what we call the genus (JEE-
nuss) and always starts with a capital letter, and the second
part of the name is the species. The scientific name for the
great white is *Carcharodon carcharias*. The combination
of these two names is always unique, so even if two species
have the same common name, they will still have different
scientific names.

Closely related species might share the same genus
name. You're a good example of that. You are a human
being (I'm assuming) and your scientific name is *Homo
sapiens*. There are over seven billion of us on the planet
but we are linked by that same scientific name. We are the
only organism to have the name *Homo sapiens*, but we are
not the only organism to have part of that name and there

are (or more accurately *were*) quite a few with the part of the name *Homo*. If we look back into our human family tree, then the Neanderthals (NEE-an-der thals) have been given the name *Homo neanderthalensis*, because they were similar to us, but not quite the same. Then there was *Homo erectus*, *Homo habilis*, *Homo naledi* and a whole bunch of others. From these names, we can see we are closely related but are different enough to be separate species.

The differences used to separate species from one another and the other levels of groupings are based on genetics, physical differences and sometimes even differences in behaviours. This is a very brief introduction to how we start to sort different species and groups from one another. Believe me, I could talk about this for hours. It's a fascinating area of biology called taxonomy (tax onno-ME) and helps scientists understand how species evolve, the relationships between different groups and how to prioritise conservation activities.

The most basic rule is that usually, as you move up the classification, a group gets broader each time, from the species (where there is only one) right up to a kingdom (although many scientists now use groups even wider than a kingdom), such as Animalia where there are over 1.5 million different animal species, or Fungi, which might have almost four million representatives. If you understand that an individual species usually sits within a group of species and that this group sits within a group called the genus, which sits within a group and that group sits within a group, and so on, then you understand the very basics of scientific classification. It's like Russian dolls: one is placed inside another, which has another inside, down to one very small doll in the centre. If you swap over dolls for the different levels of groups within taxonomy, and the smallest doll is the species itself, then you're getting there.

If you want to learn a little bit more about taxonomy now, working from the biggest group down to the smallest, it goes Kingdom, Phylum, Class, Order, Family, Genus, Species. I always remember the order by using the first letter each time to make up a silly sentence, which, for some reason, sticks in my mind better. If it helps you too, it's *King Penguins Come Out For Good Sushi*. Strange, hey? By using this classification system, you can investigate the evolution of any living (or extinct) organism on the planet.

The reason you have just had an introduction to university-level taxonomy is because *Lisowicia* has a very interesting classification. This might seem difficult to understand to start with but is important if you want to discover something incredible – where *you* came from. Looking at our own taxonomy and evolutionary family tree from the reverse point of view, it's not long before it gets confusing. In fact, we don't know for certain about many of the scientific relationships between our own species and our closest extinct ancestors, and here we're talking just a few hundred thousand years ago or less. But this is like looking at taxonomy problems under a microscope – you're only going to discover a tiny section of a tiny thing. Sometimes it's easier to look at something broadly on a larger scale, like looking at a planet through a telescope. You might see the bigger picture but now you're missing the detail. It's a bit like this with *Lisowicia* and us.

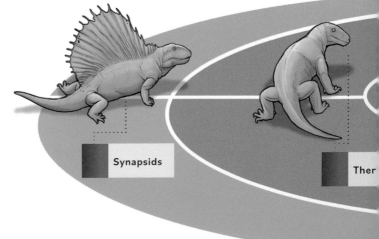

Synapsids

Ther

We have no idea about the exact relationship linking us as a species with this 200-million-year-old Triassic herbivore, but from the wider point of view, it does help us understand a bit more about our evolution as mammals as a group and how we started off, millions of years ago. It also helps us understand, quite fundamentally, the differences between mammals, birds, reptiles, amphibians and fish. You might try to be smart and say that fish breathe and swim underwater, and they have scales. But penguins also have scales and they also swim underwater. Then some fish breathe above water and some glide and some even move around on land. OK, mammals all have hair and

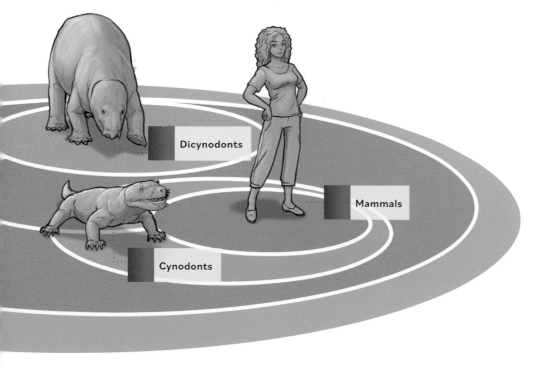

give birth to live babies. Well, whales aren't especially hairy (although they have some hairs) and other mammals like echidnas and platypuses lay eggs. And if you say that only the birds have two legs and are feathered, then well, try telling that to a *Tyrannosaurus rex* if you ever bump into one, because she was definitely not a bird.

Our definitions of different animal groups very easily become cloudy, especially when we're looking for quite detailed differences, such as the presence or absence of feathers and whether offspring are brought into the world as newborns, eggs or a combination of the two, as in some reptiles and fish. To truly understand how these groups were formed and are related to one another, we need to go way back and look at what defines them.

Let's go back to the Russian doll comparison. In the centre sits the smallest doll. In our version, this is *Lisowicia*. We need to figure out what group of animals *Lisowicia* belonged to. You're a mammal, a chicken is a bird, a shark is a fish but *Lisowicia* was none of these and belonged to a now-extinct group called the dicynodonts. In our example, the dicynodonts would be the second-smallest doll. This group was around between the Late Permian (roughly 252 million years ago) and died out just over 200 million years ago as a result of the End Triassic mass extinction. There were around 70 different types of dicynodonts, from small rat-sized species to *Lisowicia*, which was the largest. They had a beak like a turtle's and most had no teeth, except for two large tusks, and it is these that give them their name, as dicynodont means 'two dog tooth'. All the dicynodonts were herbivores.

If the dicynodonts are the second doll in our taxonomy, then they sat inside a bigger doll, as you might expect. This third doll represents a group called the therapsids (therr-ap sidz). Here's where we become a bit more relevant to the story. You may never have heard of the therapsids but you should have, because *we* are part of this group. The therapsids is a group which includes the mammals and all of our ancestors. It's a group in which all the members have limbs held directly underneath the body – like us, elephants, dogs and all the other mammals with limbs. It includes groups that are distantly related to our group, as well as extinct animals such as large-bodied herbivores like *Moschops*, with its lifestyle similar to that of hippopotamuses and a small, powerful skull capable of delivering devastating headbutts. And there were the scary, predatory gorgonopsians (gor-gon op-SEE-ans), which hunted using their large, powerful bodies and killed using their long, sabred teeth. Other groups, such as the reptiles and amphibians (which are not therapsids), have limbs which stick out from their body at a more 'sideways' angle, meaning they walk in a way which can be described more as a sprawl.

The widest group (and the fourth doll in our example) is one called the synapsids (sin-ap-sidz). This group includes the mammals and other groups with limbs, and which either lay eggs on land or develop embryos within their own body. They are more closely related to us mammals than they are to either birds or reptiles. As well as including mammals and other animals which weren't mammals but were still therapsids, such as *Moschops*, the gorgonopsians and *Lisowicia*, this is a much broader group than the therapsids and also includes our ancient relatives, even if they weren't direct ancestors.

The therapsids evolved from a group known as the pelycosaurs (pel-E CO-sors). This gets confusing quickly when you discover that even the name 'pelycosaur' seems to be going extinct because many scientists don't think it's the most accurate term. So, why do you need to know about a confusing group with a confusing name? First, although you might not have heard of the group, there's a chance you'll have heard of the most famous member of the pelycosaur group – the huge, four-legged *Dimetrodon*, with the amazing sail along its back. The second reason you might be interested is because this means you can say that way back in time (and I mean *way* back), you are very distantly related to the predatory *Dimetrodon*.

Finding things in common between us and weasels and whales is difficult enough, but identifying similarities which also allow us to include *Lisowicia* and even older animals such as *Moschops* and *Dimetrodon* in that group is even harder, and we have to identify some important but fairly basic features. One of the best ways to identify synapsids from the fossil record, from which we can't usually see how they reproduced, is to look at their skulls. Animals from the synapsid group have a hole, called the temporal fenestra, which translates as something like 'the window in the side of your head' on either side of the skull behind the eyes. Other groups such as the diapsids, which includes the majority of the reptiles and the birds and dinosaurs, have two holes on either side of their skulls, and the anapsids, which includes the turtles and tortoises, don't have any of these extra holes in the side of the skull.

If you're wondering about where the holes in the side of *your* skull are, then you're going to be disappointed because over millions of years, mammals have lost the temporal fenestra which is so important in helping classify us as part of the synapsid group. In biology, you can still belong to a group, even if you've lost the thing that helped identify you as being part of that group. Losing your school tie doesn't mean you stop belonging to your school, or misplacing a library card shouldn't mean you stop being a member of the library. Taxonomy works in the same way.

Classification such as this may seem complicated and that's partly because it *is* quite complicated, but it helps to understand how the process of classification works. If you can understand something simple like the idea that a tarantula is an example of a spider, which is an example of an arachnid, which is an example of a invertebrate, then you can understand how *Lisowicia* is an example of a dicynodont, which is an example of a therapsid, which is an example of a synapsid.

ECOLOGY

If we were to sit down and chat about any organism you name, I'd be amazed if we didn't discuss its ecology. That's because nothing in nature exists on its own but instead is the result of millions of years (and most likely hundreds of millions of years) of relationships between the climate and the weather and the physical environment, as well as the impact of predators and prey, competition between other species, the availability of essential resources such as food and a whole host of other things. This is ecology and if you understand ecology even a little bit, your understanding of nature increases massively.

Now, try imagining that species again. If it was a tarantula, then I hope you saw it emerging from its web at the base of a tree in the Brazilian forest. If it was a gorilla, perhaps you're seeing the rain-soaked mountain forests of Uganda, thick with trees, bushes and other plants, and the gorillas are eating tough giant thistle shoots, as monkeys call and brightly coloured hornbills noisily fly overhead.

When we think about a species, and especially when we want to study that species, we need to look at its ecology. To understand mountain gorillas, we'd need to look at their habitat, the climate, their diet and other species within their environment.

When we look at any prehistoric discovery, whether it's a fly trapped in amber or the freeze-dried body of a mammoth or the fossilised seed cone of a monkey-puzzle tree, then understanding the ecology of this organism is critical. For a long time, it was assumed that the Triassic period saw the arrival of the first massive herbivores on land and that these earliest 'megaherbivores' were all dinosaurs. But when we look at the ecology of *Lisowicia*, we see it wasn't only dinosaurs that reached such gigantic proportions.

Although *Lisowicia* was one of the most common animals within its environment, it definitely didn't live in isolation from other species. It shared its semi-aquatic habitat with large predators such as *Smok*, and smaller predatory dinosaurs similar to *Coelophysis* (SEE-LO FI-sis) and *Liliensternus* (lil-E-un stur-nus), which were some of the earliest members of the dinosaur group discovered so far. There were small crocodilian ancestors and various lizard-like reptiles around. The only animal closely related to *Lisowicia* was the much, much smaller *Hallautherium* (hal-au theer-EE-um), which also belonged to the group that would later evolve into the mammals.

One of the most interesting things about the ecology of *Lisowicia* is that there were no large herbivorous dinosaurs in the same area at the same time, even though they were elsewhere in Europe. *Plateosaurus* (plat-EE-O sor-us), which belonged to the group that later evolved into the four-legged, long-necked sauropods, was found across what is now central Europe, North America and Greenland.

Hitching a ride on a pair of adult *Lisowicia*, some small *coelophysid* (SEE-LO FY-sid) dinosaurs search for something to eat. As a group the dinosaurs were beginning to find success during the Triassic.

What is unknown is whether the large herbivorous dinosaurs just didn't live in this particular ecosystem and this left a 'gap' in the ecology for a big plant-eater, which allowed *Lisowicia* to grow so big and do so well, or whether there was some sort of ongoing competition and that *Lisowicia* outperformed dinosaurs such as *Plateosaurus*. Like so much in science, this is an exciting question that researchers are trying to answer.

When 🕐

Fossils from *Lisowicia* have been found in rocks from the late Triassic period. Palaeontologists have been able to age these rocks by looking at when crystals from a mineral called zircon were formed and by ageing them, they are able to estimate how old the fossil site is. From their studies, scientists believe the fossil site dates from around 208 million years ago, but that it is likely to be a few extra million years younger. This would mean that *Lisowicia* was around at the end of the Triassic and right at the time of the mass extinction event.

Where

Whereas the fossils from some species are found over a wide area, fossils from *Lisowicia* have so far been found only in Poland, in Europe. More accurately, they have been found in a series of muddy pits around a village called Lisowice near the town of Lubliniec, in the southwest of the country.

Environment

Although *Lisowicia* fossils have only been found in southwestern Poland, 200 million years ago when these animals lived, the Earth looked very different. Much of the land was gathered in huge masses, called supercontinents, and it was on the western edge of one of these, called Laurasia (lorr AY-sha), way before Poland or even Europe was around, that *Lisowicia* roamed.

The massive *Lisowicia* lived in environments that were lush, wet and swampy. One lucky lungfish grabs a free meal as a huge *Lisowicia* wades through the shallows.

Not only did the organisation of the land look unlike it does now, but the environments on the land and within the oceans were also different to what we know today. Although there was variation across the span of the Triassic, the average surface temperature of the Earth was 17°C, two degrees warmer than the average now. The land was hot and dry and if you moved away from coastal habitats towards the centre of any of the supercontinents, deserts spanned thousands and thousands of kilometres. As the largest of these supercontinents, Pangaea, started to break up, helping form the other ancient supercontinents, it meant there was more coastline in relation to the amount of land. This brought about condensation and rainfall, turning the climate wetter and more humid.

So much change going on during the time when *Lisowicia* was alive meant that there was an extensive mixture of plants, animals and habitats at the end of the Triassic period, and often quite different habitats could be found next to each another. The environment in which *Lisowicia* lived would have been lush, wet and swampy, similar to the everglades in North America today. This habitat would have been full of coniferous trees, with

their year-round needle-like leaves, as well as gingko trees, seed ferns and water-loving liverworts. There would have been slow-running rivers and features such as oxbow lakes. This dense green habitat sat alongside much drier environments, where life was not as easy for its inhabitants.

Flora and fauna

Because the Triassic period directly followed from another mass extinction, at the end of the Permian, there were lots of changes in the plants and animals found across the planet as well as in the diversity of this assortment of global flora and fauna. Some of these species would have been survivors from the previous mass extinction, whereas others made a brief appearance in the ecological 'gaps' left behind by previous extinctions.

Plants such as ginkgoes, ferns and horsetails were still present from earlier times, but during the Permian, seed-producing plants came to be incredibly successful in terrestrial habitats across Earth. In the oceans, although some important groups, such as the trilobites, were lost during the Permian mass extinction, other groups, like cephalopods (seff-a-LO pods) survived and flourished.

Ammonites (am-on ITES), diversified into the more familiar animals we know today, including octopus, squid and cuttlefish. Although in the Triassic there was not the dazzling diversity of fish we saw during the earlier Devonian period, early ichthyosaurs (ik-THEE O-sors) and the plesiosaurs (PLEE-SEE O-sors) were the first representatives of the predatory marine reptiles, which would go on to rule the world's oceans for millions of years.

On land, many examples from the group known as the cynodonts were present at the same time as *Lisowicia*. This group includes us mammals and our extinct ancestors and close relatives. The cynodonts and the dicynodonts (which includes *Lisowicia* itself) were like evolutionary cousins and shared lots of characteristics. At the time when *Lisowicia* waded along marshy riverbanks, other dicynodonts and cynodonts were thriving, but the thing which would have linked them was the constant worry that they might end up as a tasty meal for one of the most interesting and largest, yet most mysterious predators of the Triassic – *Smok*.

Growing to as much as 6m in length, *Smok* walked on two legs and had a raised tail and long, clawed forelimbs. It also had a very large, heavily built skull and long, serrated teeth. At first glance, it looked like any of the group of dinosaurs to which *Tyrannosaurus rex* belonged, but the first problem is that *Smok* existed 140 million years before the tyrannosaurs and was not part of the same group. The second problem is that despite the fact it looked like one of the most famous dinosaurs ever, scientists aren't even certain it was a dinosaur at all. Dinosaurs, birds, crocodiles and a bunch of other animals belong to a group called the archosaurs (AR-KO sors), so just because dinosaurs were archosaurs doesn't mean all archosaurs are dinosaurs.

Smok does have some parts which look very much like a dinosaur but also different bits which look more like an ancestor from the crocodile group, and other bits still which look different again. It's possible *Smok* was a dinosaur, but we are still not 100 per cent certain, so we talk about it being the largest carnivorous archosaur in Europe in the Late Triassic and Early Jurassic periods. This would mean there were no bigger land predators for millions of year, and that even the largest herbivores such as *Lisowicia* would have been at risk from attack and predation.

Smok attack! Bones from young _Lisowicia_ have been found with scrapes which perfectly match the size and shape of _Smok_ teeth.

Behaviour

Behaviour is among the most tricky but exciting things to investigate in any extinct animal. So much of what we understand about an animal's behaviour is based on actually watching that animal in action. Imagine if narwhals were extinct and all we had to understand them was their bones and the long, spiralled tusk that makes them so distinctive. We might think they used this tusk to spear fish as they swam, or maybe fought by using it like some sort of bony sword. It would be spectacular to uncover that they used the tusk as a sensory wand to detect changes in temperature, movement and even the levels of salt in the water around them. What if we never had the chance to see monkeys such as mandrills in the wild because they were extinct. We would look at their incredibly long canine teeth and assume they were for ripping their prey apart. Surely, this animal must have been a ferocious predator and not a fruit-eating monkey which uses its large canine teeth to show off to other members of its group through huge yawns? Well, because we can actually watch mandrills, we are able to say with certainty that the males use their big teeth to show off, to either warn off other males or attract females to mate. This is the challenge in trying to understand the behaviour of *Lisowicia*, or any other prehistoric animal. We have to examine the evidence we have in order to understand how they lived and how they behaved.

Many species of large herbivores are social and spend a lot of their time in groups. This is true for some dinosaurs such as the duck-billed hadrosaurs, where hundreds and hundreds of fossilised footprints show that huge herds moved together, or some Argentinian titanosaurs, which laid their eggs in massive clusters. It's also true of many herbivores alive today – think of herds of giraffes, elephants and hippopotamuses. Like these examples, *Lisowicia* may have lived in groups or spent time together throughout the year. The first piece of evidence for their social behaviour is that where fossils have been found, bones from different individuals have been discovered together.

When we reconstruct extinct species, the hardest thing to unravel is their behaviour. By looking at their prints, their bones and even their droppings, we can start to recreate how animals like *Lisowicia* fitted into their environments.

Although some of these bones were from adults and others from young animals, scientists are not sure whether this means *Lisowicia* gave any parental care. It is thought that like many of the other animals from the same group, *Lisowicia* most likely laid eggs and did not give birth to their young, as the majority of mammals do. Another strange piece of evidence for social behaviour is the discovery of what are believed to be *Lisowicia* latrines, near to where the bones have been found. Some animals defecate together in groups in a single spot, so the discovery of hundreds of fossil poos might help show they lived together and travelled around in groups.

Fossilised poo is used in palaeontology, revealing to researchers a huge amount of information on diet, adaptations and even what habitats were like. By looking at these coprolites (cop-RO LITES), scientists are able to confirm not only that *Lisowicia* was a herbivore but also that it mostly ate soft plants, such as fern leaves

and conifers. Some coprolites have been found with lots of woody material in them, which might show they ate this poor-quality food in seasons when their preferred foods weren't available.

In the *Lisowicia* story, coprolites reveal another piece in the puzzle, as *Lisowicia* remains have been found in the coprolites deposited by their main predator, *Smok*. When scientists looked at what this predator had left behind, they were able to scan their prehistoric poo, revealing crunched-up pieces of *Lisowicia* bone. *Smok* were eating *Lisowicia*, but we don't know whether they were being hunted or scavenged.

The answer becomes clearer when we learn that these bones are from juvenile *Lisowicia* and that *Smok* bite marks have been mostly found on the bones of young *Lisowicia*. If *Lisowicia* were being scavenged, these bite marks and the bones in the coprolites would be from animals at all stages of their lives, but because there seems to be a focus on young animals, it appears young *Lisowicia* were a major prey source for the largest Triassic predator in Europe.

Although *Lisowicia* were big animals, they were nevertheless still hunted. Despite not being a dinosaur, *Smok* was one of the largest predators anywhere on the planet during the Triassic.

As well as helping outsize its main predator, becoming so large allowed *Lisowicia* to eat lots of poor-quality plant material. If it takes a long time and a long digestive system to break down all that plant material, then you need a big body for big guts, making large size beneficial where there are predators but also hard-to-digest plants.

Growing big may not sound like an especially great adaptation when you compare it to other options, such as defensive weapons, wings or colour-changing camouflage, but when we look at the evolution of giant mammals and giant dicynodonts such as *Lisowicia*, we see it happens around 20 million years after the group first emerges. This shows that although becoming supersized is a slow adaptation, it is one which works again and again and has some equally hefty benefits.

GLOSSARY

Archosaurs (AR-KO sors)
A broad group of animals including birds and crocodilians, as well as extinct dinosaurs, pterosaurs and many relatives of the crocodilians.

Canine (KAY nine)
Long, pointed teeth found towards the front of the mouth in many animals. They have different uses, such as grasping prey, fighting and display.

Carnivore
Any animal which eats another animal, either by killing or scavenging them.

Conifer
Trees and shrubs that bear cones. Most conifers are 'evergreens' and do not lose their leaves in the autumn and winter.

Coprolite (cop-RO LITE)
A fossilised poo.

Cretaceous (cret-AY shuss)
The third period of time in the Mesozoic era, stretching from 145 million years ago to 66 million years ago.

Cynodonts (SINE O-donts)
A group which includes the mammals and their now-extinct close relatives.

Dicynodonts (DI SI-NO donts)
A group of extinct herbivorous terrestrial animals which usually had a set of downward-facing canines or tusks. These animals were closely related to the cynodonts but did not evolve to become the mammals.

Ecology
An area of science which studies organisms and their relationship with each other and their habitat.

Herbivore
Any animal which relies on plants for food, rather than other animals.

Mesozoic (mez-O zo-ik) era
The era which become famous for being the time when dinosaurs dominated the planet.

Palaeozoic (PAY-LEE-O zo-ik) era
A huge chunk of geological time, stretching from 541 million years ago to just over 251 million years ago. The end of the Palaeozoic was marked by the mass extinction at the end of the Permian period.

Pangaea (pan JEE-a)
A huge 'supercontinent' which was around during both the Palaeozoic and parts of the Mesozoic eras. It consisted of all the land on Earth that was visible above the surface of the oceans and started to break up during the Triassic period.

Permian (per-ME an)
A 47-million-year period of time, stretching from 298.9 million years ago to around 252.2 million years ago, which ended with the 'Great Dying' mass extinction.

Sauropodamorpha (sor-O PODE-a mor-fa)
The four-legged, long-necked, long-tailed herbivorous dinosaurs and their ancestors.

Synapsids (sin-ap-sidz)
A group of animals that includes mammals and all animals more closely related to mammals than to other groups, such as birds and reptiles.

Taxonomy (tax onno-ME)
The method in science used to classify organisms into groups, based on how related they are to one another. Taxonomy can be used to make evolutionary 'family trees'.

Tectonic (tek ton-ik) plates
The huge, slowly moving plates which form the Earth's crust and the layer beneath.

Terrestrial
On the land.

Therapsids (therr-ap sidz)
A group which includes the mammals and all of our ancestors, where the members have limbs that are held directly underneath the body, rather than sprawling out to the side, as in reptiles, for example.

Triassic (TRY-ass-ik)
The Mesozoic era was broken into three smaller periods, with the Triassic being the first and shortest of these three periods, lasting *just* 50.6 million years.

Collect all eight titles in the E✗TINCT series

One of the oldest and most mysterious animals ever described, *Hallucigenia* was a kind of sea-living, armoured worm. But it was nothing like the worms we know today. Its body was covered in spines and frills. It had claws at the end of its legs and a mouth lined with sharp teeth.

This strange animal was one of the victims of the End Ordovician mass extinction which claimed 85 per cent of the species living in the world's oceans around 443 million years ago. What could have led to this catastrophe and what caused the appearance of huge glaciers and falling sea levels, leaving many marine ecosystems dry and unable to sustain life at a time when it had only just got started?

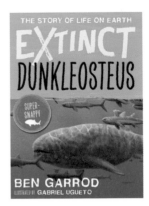

An armoured fish with a bite 10 times more powerful than that of a great white shark, *Dunkleosteus* could also snap its jaws five times faster than you can blink! It was one of the most iconic predators ever to rule the waves. What was it like to live in its shadow? And how did it become one of the many victims of the Late Devonian mass extinction around 375 million years ago?

Let's discover why this mass extinction only affected ocean life and why it went on for so long – some scientists believe it lasted for 25 million years. In a weird twist, we'll look at whether the evolution of trees on the land at that time was partly responsible for the loss of so many marine species, including *Dunkleosteus*.

Among the first arthropods – animals with jointed legs such as insects and their relatives – trilobites were around on Earth for over 300 million years and survived the first two mass extinctions. There were once at least 20,000 species but all disappeared in the devastating End Permian mass extinction around 252 million years ago.

We'll look at why land animals were affected this time as well as those in the sea. An incredible 96 per cent of marine species went extinct and an almost equally terrible 70 per cent of life on land was wiped out in what is known as the 'Great Dying'. This was the closest we've come to losing all life on Earth and the planet was changed forever.

Weighing as much as three adult elephants and as long as a bus, *Tyrannosaurus rex* was one of the mightiest land predators that has ever lived. It had the most powerful bite of any dinosaur and dominated its environment. But not even the biggest dinosaurs were a match for what happened at the end of the Cretaceous, about 66 million years ago.

What happened when an asteroid travelling at almost 40,000km/h crashed into Earth? Creating a shockwave that literally shook the world, its impact threw millions of tonnes of red-hot ash and dust into the atmosphere, blocking out the sun and destroying 75 per cent of life on Earth. Any living thing bigger than a fox was gone and this fifth global mass extinction meant the end of the dinosaurs as we knew them.

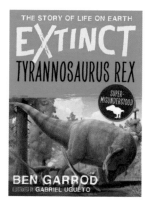

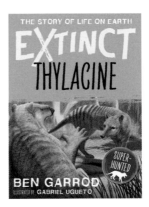

A giant marine predator, megalodon grew up to an incredible 18m – longer than three great white sharks, nose to tail. This ferocious monster had the most powerful bite force ever measured. It specialised in killing whales by attacking them from the side, aiming for their heart and lungs.

But, like more than 50 per cent of marine mammals and many other creatures, megalodon disappeared in the End Pliocene mass extinction around 2.5 million years ago. We'll find out why this event affected many of the bigger animals in the marine environment and had an especially bad impact on both warm-blooded animals and predators.

The thylacine, also known as the Tasmanian tiger, is one of a long list of species, ranging from sabre-toothed cats to the dodo, that have been wiped out by humans. The last wild thylacine was shot in 1930 and the last captive thylacine alive died in a zoo in 1936.

We'll explore the mass extinction we are now entering and how we, as a species, have the power to wipe out other species – something no other single species is able to do. Who are the winners and losers and why might it take over seven million years to restore mammal diversity on Earth to what it was before humans arrived?

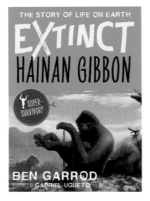

One of the most endangered animals on our planet, the Hainan gibbon is also one of our closest living relatives. Family groups of these little primates live in the trees on an island off the south coast of China and they feed on leaves and fruit.

But the gibbons are now in serious trouble because of the effects of human population increase around the world and habitat destruction. Without action, this animal might soon be extinct and need a dagger after its name. What can we all do to help stop some of our most interesting, iconic and important species from going extinct?

BEN GARROD is Professor of Evolutionary Biology and Science Engagement at the University of East Anglia. Ben has lived and worked all around the world, alongside chimpanzees in Africa, polar bears in the Arctic and giant dinosaur fossils in South America. He is currently based in the West Country. He broadcasts regularly on TV and radio and is trustee and ambassador of a number of key conservation organisations. His debut six-book series *So You Think You Know About... Dinosaurs?* and *The Chimpanzee and Me* are also published by Zephyr.

GABRIEL UGUETO is a scientific illustrator, palaeoartist and herpetologist based in Florida. For several years, he was an independent herpetologist researcher and authored papers on new species of neotropical lizards and various taxonomic revisions. As an illustrator, his work reflects the latest scientific hypotheses about the external appearance and the behaviour of the animals, both extinct and extant, that he reconstructs. His illustrations have appeared in books, journals, magazines, museum exhibitions and television documentaries.

Zephyr is an imprint of Head of Zeus.
At Zephyr we are proud to publish books
you can read and re-read time and time
again because they tell a brilliant story
and because they entertain you.

 @_ZephyrBooks

 @_zephyrbooks

 HeadofZeusBooks

readzephyr.com

www.headofzeus.com

ZEPHYR